BIGFOOT FOR WOMEN

www.youtube.com/watch
?v=FCj_C-Yb3xI

BIGFOOT FOR WOMEN

AMY PICKWORTH

[poems]

ORANGE MONKEY PUBLISHING

This is for my mother,
who deserves to have a book
dedicated to her,
and for my father,
who doesn't.

Bigfoot is here

Published by Orange Monkey Publishing
Copyright © 2014 by Amy Pickworth
Printed by PubGraphics.com
ISBN: 978-0-9894771-6-1

Acknowledgments
Grateful thanks to the following journals, where
some of these poems were published first: "Revelations"
[Discover an ice man instead], "This geography of
bigfoot," "Koko turns a copy of Keats's death mask,"
and "Long Winter" appeared in *CATACOMB,* Summer 2014.
"Darkling, I listen" was published at Ink Node on
July 24, 2013, www.inknode.com/piece/1832-amy-pickworth-
darkling-i-listen, and "Timeline" appeared in *New
Ohio Review,* Issue 12, Fall 2012.

Cover image adapted from *Proud Maisie*
by Frederick Sandys

Book design by Lucinda Hitchcock

contents

----

from the author

A number of internet addresses are included in
this manuscript, but the internet, like any healthy
forest, is constantly changing. New things spring
up as others die off. The links included here are
breadcrumbs on the path. Some might be gone by
the time you get there, but this is also how the forest
works. You'll find another way. Or if you are truly
lost, email BigfootforWomen@gmail.com and I will
send you something to get you unlost again.

acknowledgments

I would like to thank the writers and musicians who populate this book and then some, for bringing me joy and teaching me things I didn't always know I needed to know. This includes Heidi Lynn Staples, who isn't cited directly but whose work "Take Care Fake Bear Torque Cake" showed me something about the wildness of language.

I am grateful for my many friends, in particular Julie Gearan, Jean Harper, Lucy Hitchcock, Mary Beth Meehan, Eve Müller, Lynda Fleet Perry, Maggie Smith, and Tina Tryforos, whose encouraging words were important in the early days of this manuscript. I'm especially grateful to Lucy for her beautiful, thoughtful design and to Tina for making author photos almost fun. Special thanks also to David Baker, a remarkable teacher; to Darcie Dennigan, who said it might be cool to keep the hyperlinks; and to Terence Winch, who hired me a long time ago as an editor and turned me into a writer. Enormous gratitude to Larry Eby and Matt Hart for saying yes, and also to my husband for saying yes in an entirely different way.

In Ted Berrigan's deliberately loose and bewilderingly
lively homage to, and translation of, Arthur Rimbaud's ars
poetica, "The Drunken Boat," the poem's eighth stanza is
rendered like this:

```
I've seen skies split with light, and night,
and surfs, currents, water-spouts; I know
what evening means, and doves, and I have seen
what other men sometimes have thought they've seen.
```

Thinking about writing this introduction, I was reminded of
"The Drunken Boat"—both its phantasmagoria of nearly
impossible images of the poetic temperament and process,
and also of Berrigan's translation of this stanza in particular.
Why? Because Amy Pickworth has seen things other men
(and women) have only thought they've seen. That's right.
She has seen Bigfoot; "bigfoot is/ bigfoot is alive/ bigfoot is
here," she writes. But, interestingly, he doesn't look anything
like what you might expect, and at the same time he's
everything you might expect, and more: a father, a monster,
an absence, the Other. He's every boy you've ever kissed,
the boogeyman, the stars in a molten and unforgivable sky.
Your grandmother's disgust. A distant relative, an ancestor.

An unpredictable animal you wouldn't let in the house, but that might break in anyway. With Bigfoot, the scenery is always shifting, and so too the grounds of our understanding. Sasquatch. The Pig Man. Bastard.

To read *Bigfoot for Women* is to travel a long, long distance across time and space. Chaucer makes an appearance here. So too John Keats. There's Patti Smith singing Paul Simon, *Mutual of Omaha's Wild Kingdom*, Karen Carpenter, Bob Dylan, Jane Goodall, the Velvet Underground and Nico, Koko the gorilla doing sign language while watching a sad movie on TV. And in the most contemporary cameos of all, Matthew Zapruder and Maggie Nelson show up. Bigfoot's family tree it seems is very, very large indeed. Amy Pickworth is part of it. You're probably part of it. Read on, and you'll see.

Bigfoot for Women is a journey unlike any I've ever before had the pleasure of taking with/in a book of poems. Like the Bigfoot creature itself, the book is elusive, but nearly constantly allusive as well—in motion, kinetic, boiling over with memory, history, human nature, and love. Follow its links—choose your own adventure. Notice its formal variation—pantoum, erasure, interview, timeline, prose poem, mix-tape—and in all of this its willingness to leave out what it must, while simultaneously including seemingly EVERYTHING. It is a work of art in 4-D (the fourth dimension being that of time and motion, of course). As a book, it constantly kicks the reader out, but always provides instructions for getting back in: think about this, Google that, reflect on an image of Cocteau's Beast. In this way, *Bigfoot for Women* is an instruction manual, an exposée, a guided tour of the mysteries, a hunt for the "great/ unknowable, unreliable heart" of Bigfoot himself. In the process, you will no doubt choose and/or come to know your very own Bigfoot. It turns out that everybody has many of them. (And while ostensibly this is Bigfoot for women, it

must be noted that "men" is contained in the word "women."
Anyway, this book's for you, guys, as much as anybody.)

Am I a Bigfoot? Are you? Yes. And that's not all bad.
Bigfoot's in all of us and everywhere; as this book shows,
"To know Bigfoot/ is to know many things about secrets,/
including ways you can hide your own tracks." But it's also
about knowing/facing your own secrets, which is so much
more complicated—so much harder—than it sounds. I bet
when you read this you'll reflect on your self and all the wild
forces that have shaped you.

In short, I read a lot of books, and a lot of them I actually
like, but this one I love. It makes me want to grow thick fur
all over my body and go galumphing through the forest like
a grizzly-elk-man-thing. For women and men and everybody.
It makes me want you to grow fur all over your body, too—
then post the results on Youtube, along with your own wild-
eyed review of this book. Once you've seen things that other
men other women have only thought they've seen, there's
no going back. You've gotta make a run for it. Tell everybody:
Bigfoot is here. Bigfoot is real. Bigfoot is awesome. A wonderful
promise in the wilderness of contemporary life.

and here...

Part One

This is not to say that the non-human world is somehow unreal or a mere figment of our imaginations—far from it. But the way we describe and understand that world is so entangled with our own values and assumptions that the two can never be fully separated. What we mean when we use the word "nature" says as much about ourselves as about the things we label with that word. As the British literary critic Raymond Williams once famously remarked, "The idea of nature contains, though often unnoticed, an extraordinary amount of human history."

-William Cronon, Uncommon Ground (1996)

- - -

This may be hard to believe but listen:
every word I'll tell you is true. *He is*
out there, behind Cabin G, making out
with all the girls, prowling dim back yards and
planned communities. He's what our mothers
warned us about: dangerous young feral
Brando and butterstick werewolf Brando
all rolled into one.
                              Okay, a girl from
Cabin G laughs, cracks her gum, then launches
the charade, turning, wrapping her arms tight
around her waist, flopping soft in his clutch.

We need a break from this ruined country.
Some kind of pure place to stash our over-
flow of longing for one almost-true thing.

Suppose[1] I shredded a Kleenex and said
that I had fallen in love with Bigfoot.
Or the idea that Bigfoot is out there
wandering around and we can't find him.
Something something something about his great
unknowable, unreliable heart.
baBoombaBoomBoombaBoomBoombaBoombabababaBoombabaBoombaBoomba.

- - -

Track 1: www.youtube.com/watch?v=HBxC-PDPIIk.[2]
Please do not focus on the Patti Smith
montage or think about how she is cool,
although yes, she is. Listen to the words,
which, you're right, technically are Paul Simon's.

Think about baboon hearts and feel grateful
there's a real creature called the bleeding heart
baboon. Go here if you want more on this,
feel free to quit watching if you get bored:
www.youtube.com/watch?v=E0iDOey9G5w.[3]

Understand that you'll loop back to this song.

---

1. www.amazon.com/Bluets-Maggie-Nelson/dp/1933517409#reader_1933517409.
   Or take a shortcut by going to tinyurl.com/lajyttf.
2. Or tinyurl.com/m8hce7c.
3. Or tinyurl.com/mejdwow.

\- - -

I wrote to the cryptozoologist
a while ago and asked *What do you think*
it means, that we want Bigfoot to exist?
Or put another way, what does what we
believe about Bigfoot say about us?

He wrote me back. *Just buy one of my books.*

I wrote him back. I said *I did, but you*
don't talk about any of this. Why
is it that we want Bigfoot to exist?

This marked the end of our correspondence.

Vacuuming the carpet, I think about
Bigfoot, about aliens and belief
and how we end up doing all the things
we mocked our mothers mercilessly for.
It's easier to love dead anything.

They say the Appalachian Trail is a
Bigfoot highway, which you think sounds funny
until the day one comes through your back door
and drags your family away. And which one
of your lost saints is gonna save you then?

bigfoot is real
bigfoot is not a political symbol
bigfoot is sasquatch
bigfoot is watching you
bigfoot is alive and well in boston
bigfoot is phenomenon
bigfoot is no tall tale to true believers in ohio
bigfoot is
bigfoot is alive
bigfoot is here
bigfoot is obviously much more similar to humans
bigfoot is living in minnesota
bigfoot is so popular around the world that there have been several
      bigfoot
bigfoot is an ape/hominid that is rumored to exist in the northwestern
      us and western canada
bigfoot is a living prehistoric ape or early human
bigfoot is the unknowable masculine
bigfoot is on hand with which to compare hair
bigfoot is "the honey island swamp monster" which has been reported
      to have been seen in the southeast swamp areas of louisiana
bigfoot is a large cryptid
bigfoot is the answer to the huge demand for a rugged
bigfoot is not a "missing link" but is most probably descended from the
      giant ape gigantopithecus
bigfoot is remarkable
bigfoot is for real
bigfoot is not a bear and for many reasons
bigfoot is grendel
bigfoot is inhabiting the state of ohio or pennsylvania
bigfoot is being carried on in california
bigfoot is extremely shy
bigfoot is supposed to live are mostly highly inaccessible or covered
      with a dense vegetation that prevents any spotting from the sky
bigfoot is having an affair with my mother

bigfoot is seen again
bigfoot is not one of them
bigfoot is there
bigfoot is alive at least in our consciousness
bigfoot is an assistant professor in the department of pediatrics
bigfoot is documented as a native american mythical creature
bigfoot is probably the coolest place on planet earth
bigfoot is a huge hair covered hominid that roams the dense forests of the
       pacific northwest
bigfoot is real if it isn't happening in their own backyard
bigfoot is seen in every possible location throughout the north american
       continent
bigfoot is a peaceloving creature
bigfoot is not alone
bigfoot is in 1997 ontwikkeld om met een goed off
bigfoot is believed to reside
bigfoot is out there
bigfoot is more of the pacific northwest variety
bigfoot is generally reported to be a shy
bigfoot is finally resolved
bigfoot is the answer to your requests for a rugged
bigfoot is just one of the many interesting investigations that we pursue
bigfoot is pretty harmless
bigfoot is and if there is any physical evidence that one exists
bigfoot is mere myth remain in their cynicism
bigfoot is the footprints that have been found that some say belong to
       none other than monster
bigfoot is the only way to go

Track 2: www.youtube.com/watch?v=GFQWflbG4h4 [4]

This has concentric circles pooling out,
but if you want to, google images
for "cocteau belle et la bête" while it plays.

You might consider watching the whole film.
French 1940s Bigfoot is Bigfoot
all the same. It just says *I am your door,*
I am your mirror, I have a good heart
but I am a monster all in pretty
black-and-white French superweirdness instead.

Note the sagittal crest and prominent
brow ridge. The abundant, presumably
soft fur. You may also appreciate
the costumes and sets, which are very nice.

Friend Koko the gorilla on Facebook.

4. Or tinyurl.com/m5gnk6w.

Okay. So this is how it always goes.

The you at the table is you. You are eight. You are also your mother (who is thirty-eight), the table, the indoor-outdoor carpet stamped with a print resembling something like linoleum or stained glass. You are the faucet and the sink wiped clean and the old wooden cabinet blocked closed by the installation of the newer plastic cabinet. You are also, on the other side of the sink, this cabinet's twin, which once, briefly, housed a rat dopey with poison. You are the window and the three stairs, which creak, each sloping slightly into the center like a depressed tongue. You lead to the back door. You are the back door. And you are Bigfoot, who walks past the window you, through the door you, and picks up your mother you. The Bigfoot who carries her into the back yard, past the slack tetherball you, the blooming peony yous, and across the open field you. Bigfoot then disappears into the woods, the woods that are also you.

Darkling, I listen[5]

My chest hurts and it's fucking cold out here
but I like it. I've spent hours waiting,
years, but I have never seen a bigfoot.
I keep listening though. Keep my eyes open.
It's lonely and I can't feel my feet but
I'm happy thinking he might be here too.
You know my hair went white up in this tree?
Twenty years of dressing to match the leaves.
You hear that bird? Cardinal. Calling his wife.
Listen: Now she's calling him back again.

God I could use a beer. I miss drinking.
Eight years sober, but I still remember
how it tasted—like cold summer sunshine,
like baseball playoffs with you in the lead.
What I wouldn't give for a beer sometimes.
Christ, for a six-pack, that soft warm fadeout.

Fadeout's the problem, though—don't remember
a lot, and what I do is unhappy.
Little kids cry all the time, so I'd go
to the bar and watch men drink till they're numb
then feel bad that they've pissed it all away.
Meanwhile my wife lost weight, went back to work.
My kids watched too much TV, lost their fear
of the stove, made their own grilled cheese and soup.
Microwaved their own chicken nugget things.
Then one bright blue winter day my wife said
she'd fallen in love with somebody else.

Yeah, if I ever found a bigfoot then
I might just have to run right off with him.

5. www.poetryfoundation.org/poem/173744, or tinyurl.com/m2obfbb.

Wouldn't that be something? Flowers blooming
all around me and my buddy Bigfoot.
We'd know each tree, the plants that you can eat.
Hiking days along cool ferny creek beds,
making camp every night, the stars glinting
up above us like little fairy lights.

We've lost all our light now and I can't see
a goddamn thing but that wind smells like snow.
Too cold for rain.

Darkling, I listen and listening can hear
almost everything. All the ancient groans
of barns going down, stripped of their boards, boards
that'll be sold to the contractors who get
paid extra to make new buildings look old.
I hear the farmer's granddaughter vacuum
the carpet after today's funeral.
They'll be putting his field on the market,
will sell it to a different contractor
who'll dig twenty holes and drop a cheap house
on top of every one. It makes me sad.

Sad. That word. I'm fucking sick of being
sad, like I'm the last one left of something.
Hell yes I am mad. At them, at those birds
that I can't name. Stand up for yourself, tree!
I have grown tired of watching these people
walk all over you, delicate grasses.

I remember running through the grass, growl
of the tractor calling us. Running fast
to avoid the snakes, finally reaching
open fields, bare feet pressing deep down in

the warm fresh dirt. Stand still and you could feel
the dirt warming your blood, and this warm blood
traveling up your legs. We were looking
for arrowheads turned over by the plow.

When Bigfoot or anything else goes bad,
then more bad things happen. It's that simple.
You saw *Planet of the Apes*. They are just
like us. Wondering if they have souls, why
they're always such disappointing lovers.
They too are drawn by the glitter and swank
of Christmastime, but then feel bad about
the excess, the lack of good will toward men
and a decent recycling program.
They have no idea how to make money.

So don't give bigfoots typewriters or guns.
Don't let them live under an overpass
or inside your hat.

- - -

www.thetimes.co.uk/tto/news/world/americas/article3626431.ece[6]

Now ponder the resemblances between
the Ikea monkey and Cocteau's beast:
proclivities for oversized collars
and troubled relationships with the world.

---

6. Or tinyurl.com/bnrek19.

When you can't get Bigfoot out of your mind when you are dreaming, then what this usually suggests is the idea that you want to be more elusive with your emotions. You feel as if you are too upfront with many aspects of yourself and it has hurt you in the past. Thus, you now strive to hide away your feelings on many subjects and try to keep your emotions from others in the hopes that you will not be made fun of for your beliefs. This can be healthy or unhealthy depending on the type of person that you are. But for the most part, we need emotional expression. There are sometimes when it is okay to bottle up your feelings, but you need not do this all the time, or it will lead to outbursts and feelings of uselessness and sadness later on in life.

If you dream that you see Bigfoot then what this means is that you feel as if you are not being believed in real life. People do not put their trust in you as much as you would like. When you see Bigfoot and try to tell someone else about it, their first reactions is immediately doubt, and why is that? It is because most people doubt the legitimacy of Bigfoot as a real creature and seek to cast doubt on the idea that he could be. On a related note, a dream like this could also result from the idea that you feel as if you are just generally not being taken seriously when you come up with ideas or assertions. Try to be a bit more assertive and convincing about what you believe. It is the only way that you will succeed in life and get people to treat you with more respect.

If you dream that you are hunting bigfoot and cannot find him, then what this suggests is that you cannot make your mind up about something in your life, but you are not quite sure why. This dream comes about when you are going through that paradoxical period where you feel as if you have something that you need to accomplish

or something you need to do before you can move ahead, but you aren't quite sure what that is, and can't seem to get any idea of how to find out what it is.

---

7. Or tinyurl.com/mr33d7n.

the human mind is not as perfect as people seem to think.

---

http://www.youtube.com/watch?v=4NmCmfdFAhQ[8]

Think about this for a while, then practice saying *Yeti hair* like Jane Goodall does.

8. Or tinyurl.com/mt7d25k.

King Kong is in constant danger

You're a pretty tough guy, but if beauty gets you
—the voice trails off. You are in Africa, watching
as blossoms are arranged in a young girl's afro.
The beast (your beast) tears Fay Wray down from the altar,
the crowd, always with the torches and pointy sticks,
goes wild. *Will you just look at the size of those tracks.*

Moving on. A dinosaur is shot. We march past
the body, take notes as Kong pries a T. rex face
apart, fake blood pumping over fake reptile skin.
He snaps a giant snake to the ground, dismembers
that pterodactyl, but this is okay because
you know it's not safe to be a primate. Your beast
rolls his eyes, beats his chest, removes Fay Wray's clothing.
Gives her a tickle. Picks his nose. The villagers
get restless, so Kong bites a man in half, grinds one
other into the mud. He too can be cruel.
He belongs to the people, not to the wisecracking
filmmakers who say *he's been king of this world but*
we will teach him fear.

To do this, you all head to New York, where he's named
the world's eighth wonder and receives a good turnout.
Matrons come in fingerwaves and triple strands of pearls,
Fay up there in her mink and orchids, Carl Denham
in his top hat. Twelve men met horrible deaths and
he was a god in the world that he knew but now
he comes to our civilization merely to
satisfy your curiosity. Understand
that the writer hates his audience (we assume
the writer is a man) as you pity your beast,
bound by chains of chrome steel.

And then he's free! Chomping a banker! Reaching in
a window for one starlet, ogling another,
all googoo eyes and giant minstrel face. She worms
away in her satin gown. He moves on, rips up
some train tracks out of spite, punches a darkened car,
clambers to his perch, and he is nothing like what
you remember:

He is tiny—three, maybe four stories at most.
Trapped, biplanes ratatatting away, he touches
fingertips to chest, examines the bloody stream.
Now he's losing steam fast. Fay is silhouetted
by everything deco as Cole Porter tickles
the ivories in a penthouse tower across town.
Orphans shill newspapers on the corner below.

You don't need to watch his awkward descent, banging
hard against every stepped-back granite ledge. You know
it wasn't the airplanes that got him.

- - -

http://pinktentacle.com/2010/03/human-faced-dog/[9]
Read everything on this page. Everything.

Oh my god. Japanese human-faced dogs,
dead office workers. You love it too much.

Add *Invasion of the Bodysnatchers*
to your Netflix queue, but you don't have to
watch it now—just admire the still of the
old man's head on the boxer-dog body.
Make this your new Facebook profile picture.

This is probably enough for today.

---

9. Or tinyurl.com/yl753gz.

The you at the table is you. You are eight. You are also your mother, the table, the vase of pink and white peonies, the fake saloon doors, the stained-glass carpet. You are the faucet and the sink wiped clean and the cabinet under the sink that once, briefly, housed the poisoned rat that made your mother scream until your brother killed it with a baseball bat. You are the hum of the fridge. You are the window and the three stairs, which creak, each sloping slightly into the center like a depressed tongue. Ahh, you are the door. And you are Bigfoot, who walks past the window you, through the door you, and picks up your mother you. The Bigfoot who carries her into the back yard and disappears into the woods, which you've since read is the best kind of forest outside of someplace in China and far better than this part of Ohio deserves.

Discover an ice man instead. Find his
driver's license, date him to the blizzard
of '78. Caucasian, twenty
years old, 165 pounds, 5´10˝. Found
curled in a mound of dirty snow. He is
wearing a sheepskin-lined jacket, no hat.

As he thaws, water beads on his shiny
polyester shirt, which is printed with
an autumn waterfall scene. Decide that
your ice man liked to be near the water.

With him are his tools—two dimes for the phone,
sixteen dollars, a guitar pick, a stick
of gum, a couple of Quaaludes now paste
in his wallet, his wallet printed with
the circle of a condom. No tattoos,
no piercings, but his faint tan lines reveal
that he worked construction this past summer.

It will be summer again—Nancy Drew
in *Playboy*, Sid and Nancy still alive
and naked on the gold record they shot
out into space.[10] Another good season
for Nolan Ryan, Carl Yastrzemski.

Eulogize him by awkwardly saying
he barely arrived at the beginning
of us, and went forth bravely at the worst
time of year, and on such a long journey.

10. www.youtube.com/watch?v=Axj1CVG6udE, or tinyurl.com/mo8g5bc.

- - -

Make a chart detailing what every call
might mean. Also rhythmic pounding and grunts.
Don't look them in the eye. Make lots of noise.
Run (or *don't run*). Research what you should do
if you encounter a bear or lion.

Watch a bunch of Bigfoot stuff on YouTube.[11]

11. www.youtube.com/results?search_query=bigfoot&sm=3, or tinyurl.com/m8tdfrg.

\- - -

Struggle with artificiality,
with the word *authentic*. Think about that
baby hummingbird, napping on the pink
acrylic blanket, just like a human
girl baby.

Hate Thoreau just a little when you learn
his mom packed his lunch, did all his laundry.

www.youtube.com/watch?v=EWxCM6llL60 [12]

- - -

Koko signs her thousand words, understands
a thousand more, asks to see her keeper's
breasts. More keepers complain, file a lawsuit.
Some other keepers say she meant *people*,
not *nipples*. Koko wouldn't be that crude.

- - -

Wish that the story of Koko drawing
the bars of her cage were true, but it's not.

---

12. Or tinyurl.com/3w4hmeb.

BkIV:8–66 On Locating a Forest Ape [13]

To find the entrance of an ape lair, look first
for where no wind can enter (since the winds
carry their strong scent) and where no sheep or butting kids
leap about among the bluebells, because these will have already
been eaten. Let the bright-colored lizard with scaly back
and the bee-eater and other birds and the mountain people
with blood-stained hands be your guides.
Look for an area where the bees are flying.
Let there be clear springs nearby, and pools green with moss,
and a little stream sliding through the grass, where
in the springtime their young might enjoy freedom, and
a neighboring bank may tempt them to leave the heat,
and a tree in the way hold them in its sheltering leaves.
If you wish to draw them to a place, whether the water flows
or remains still, throw willows across the center, and large stones,
so that it's full of bridges where they can rest, and spread
their long arms and recline in the summer sun.
Let green rosemary, and wild thyme with far-flung fragrance,
and a wealth of strongly scented savory flower around them,
and let beds of violets drink from the trickling spring.
Their lairs themselves will have narrow entrances,
whether they're seamed from hollow bark
or woven from pliant osiers. If rumor's true they also like
homes in tunneled hiding-places underground, and are
often found deep in the hollows, and in caverns of decaying trees.
They keep warm with clay smoothed by their fingers
round their drafty homes, a few leaves on top.
Don't hew too near these homes, or roast blushing
crabs on your hearth nearby, or trust too well the deep marsh
where there's a strong smell of skunk, or where hollow rock
rings when struck and an echoed voice rebounds.

---

13. www.poetryintranslation.com/PITBR/Latin/VirgilGeorgicsIV.htm#_Toc534524375,
    or tinyurl.com/mr4v3w5.

But gentle going, when the golden sun has driven winter
under the earth, and unlocked the heavens with summer light,
you will find them wandering through the glades and forests,
grazing the bright flowers and sipping the surface of the streams.
With a delightful sweetness, they cherish their lives
and their young. So, should you look up to find a shrewdness
of apes floating across the meadows, looking
toward the radiant sky through the clear summer air
and marveling at dark clouds drawn along by the wind,
take note: they are continually searching for sweet waters
and leafy canopies. Scatter the scents I demanded,
bruised balm and humble herbs, and make only a tinkling sound
or shake Cybele's cymbals around, for she is their deity too,
and they'll settle themselves near you and rest and bury
themselves, as they do, in the deepest forest cradle they can find.

When I was a boy, some 20-something years ago, my daddy and I were fishing bush hooks at night in the St. Marys River a little north of the swamp. We were in a little john boat and had a flashlight lantern to see by. We had paddled up into a small lake just off the main river when I heard something that scared me. I heard something BIG tromping through the woods between us and the main river. It sounded like it walked on two legs by the rhythm of its strides. It paused for a second and then made a gigantic SPLASH! The boat rocked as the waves from the splash reached us. I was terrified, but my daddy had the flashlight in one hand and a big catfish on a bush hook in the other and I couldn't see anything behind me where the noise was. After a few seconds of splashing, I heard whatever it was climb up the opposite bank and continue crashing on down the river bank away from us. I don't know for sure what it was, but I think it was too big and too heavy to have been a deer. I suppose it could have been a bear, but it sounded like it was tromping through on two legs and I'm sure it could see us and wasn't fearful in the least to jump into the water almost on top of us. I was more concerned with staying away from that area the next day than I was of trying to look for any tracks from the night before. A few months later, I rode my bicycle down to the same general area and walked down the riverbank to fish a little. There were no cars or other people there when I arrived. After a little while, I heard some commotion back towards the landing where I had left my bike. I walked out to find my bike knocked over and my tackle box rolled. I didn't see anyone or any vehicles, but in the mud near my bike was big footprints pressed down deep. I didn't recognize them as bear prints, but they seemed to be oversized man tracks. I gathered up my stuff and half rode and half ran the mile or so back home! That cured me of wanting to go fishing down there for quite a while.

---

14. Or tinyurl.com/lqxqhgo.

This geography of bigfoot[15]
is all wrong, you guys—

whether bigfoots are out there
what we think we are
where they started out
where they want to go.

Half the Midwestern bigfoots
did time in New York
the other half in Oregon.

The ones out in California
were wounded elsewhere.
When they feel better
or can't find suitable cover
they'll go back where
they came from.

This is America:
You're driven out from where you're born
you make the best of it
as far from home as you need to go
you die somewhere in between.

The only geography of Bigfoot
is the Appalachian Trail
the Pacific Northwest Trail
the Bigfoot highways.
Ubi patria ibi bene
or *ubi bene ibi patria*
or something something about
refusing the bread of nostalgia,
not that there's much of it left.

We came, we saw, we dreamt
with unclosed lids
about our birthplaces and learned:
There's a Bigfoot for everyone.
Some of them came from very far.

Maps don't help much.

15. www.poetryfoundation.org/poem/242560, or tinyurl.com/m76ag5x.

Part Two

*All truth passes through three
stages: first, it is ridiculed;
second, it is violently opposed;
and third, it is accepted as
self-evident.*

-Arthur Schopenhauer or www.youtube.com/watch?v=FCj_C-Yb3xI
[tinyurl.com/kudjcrp].

Grapefruit hand cream madeleine [16]

And once again I had recognized
the smell of canned ham
baked in a decoction of cloves
and frozen concentrated orange juice
which my mother used to make us
   (although I did not know
    and will long postpone understanding
    why this memory made me so happy).

Immediately the old white house
   on the two-lane highway
   where her room was
   where we lived with our dogs
   beside the mobile-home lot

rose up like the scenery of a theater.

16. http://books.google.com/books?id=5woenbbAp-8C&pg=PA63&dq=%22where+her+room+was%22+proust+remembrance&hl=en&sa=X&ei=Me1ZUvX6CoTqkAeX7oCgBA&ved=0CEMQ6AEwAA#v=onepage&q=%22where%20her%20room%20was%22%20proust%20remembrance&f=false, or tinyurl.com/kay3fkt.

How long did it take to figure it out?
Darcie asks. The bar's a slo-mo stampede.
I find the whites of her animal eyes
her irises gone flat in this red light
and she is amused. Dime | dime | smiley mouth
is how her face would go if you wrote it.

A while, I say. *Longer than it should have.*

The you at the table is you. You are eight. You are also your mother, who at thirty-eight is still a smoker and so a cigarette is burning in the ashtray. Your mother you is at the stove, flipping grilled cheese you. Tomato soup you is heating over a second blue flame you. You are at the table, which is you, just like the fake saloon doors and the indoor-outdoor carpet stamped with a print to resemble something like linoleum. You are the faucet and the sink wiped clean and the window and the three creaking stairs that lead to the back door. You are the door. And you are Bigfoot, who walks past the window you, through the door you, and picks up your mother you. There is no sound as this happens, but Bigfoot turns his face to you with eyes like coins and you think there is something being conveyed here about not being afraid to be alive and lonely in your body.

You once tried to explain this dream to a babysitter who is now long dead. She was a virgin in her sixties and kept a scrap of the airship *Shenandoah* in a trunk in her big strange house.[17] When you drove by last year, a Confederate flag was flapping in the window of what had been her bedroom, the bedroom with two twin beds pushed together. There was a brittle rubber Donald Duck soap dish that floated in the bath.

You tried to tell her how it is you can make yourself feel very strange when you think about how this, right now, is one moment *and see this is the next moment   and the next.*   And that time just continues and you don't even have to do anything, and it must be that way even when you're dead.

She tells you this is good, that you should think about this every day of your life.

---

17. www.google.com/maps/@39.937387,-82.018162,3a,75y,87.9h,90t/data=!3m4!1e1!3m2
!1sDIZUVkrUxKf0zreavFv-_Q!2e0, or tinyurl.com/kofmu4t.

From *The Compact Edition of the Oxford English Dictionary,* which comes with a magnifying glass and smells like old-man basement.

Bastard

A *sb.* 1. One begotten and born out of wedlock; an illegitimate or natural child.

2. *fig.*

3. A mongrel, an animal of inferior breed.

4. A sweet kind of Spanish wine, resembling muscadel in flavour, sometimes applied to any kind of sweetened wine.

5. A kind of cloth of inferior or mixed quality, or unusual make or size.

6. A kind of war-vessel, a variety of galley.

7. A species of cannon, also called a *bastard culverin.*

8. A large sail used in the Mediterranean when there is little wind.

9. A particular size of paper.

10. *Sugar-refining.* A. An impure coarse brown sugar, made from the refuse syrup of previous boilings. B. A large mould into which sugar is drained.

11. *Comb.,* as *bastard-bearing, -bellied, -like.*

B *adj.* 1. Born out of wedlock.

2. Mongrel, hybrid, of inferior breed.

3a. *fig.* Illegitimate, inferior, unrecognized.

3b. *Bastard branch* or *slip*: a shoot or sucker springing of its own accord from the root of a tree, or where not wanted.

4. *fig.* Not genuine; counterfeit, spurious; debased, adulterated, corrupt.

5. Having the appearance of, somewhat resembling; an inferior or less proper kind of: esp. in scientific nomenclature applied to things resembling, but not identical with, the species which legitimately bears the name.

Two months pregnant, you're getting a massage
from Angela. She's a British hippie.

She circles the Tibetan singing bowls
on your back, waves arcing across the room,
air shimmering hard, and says *Lotta grief
come off you with that.   Family.   Father.*
And you say *That might be true.* She goes on
You need to put these old things behind you.

You're just a little alien, darling.
Truth is, you simply needed to get here.
You don't need this family. And honestly:
they've never needed you. So don't look back.
Start putting all your energy in this
lovely little pinky-orangey baby.

Now let's call you a cab back home. You can
make some tea and get under the duvet.

- - -

Track 3: www.youtube.com/watch?v=_BrSVOOK610 (start at :50).[18]

In this song everyone's an alien,
which is nice. And if Karen Carpenter's
body makes you feel sad, that's okay too.

---

18. Or tinyurl.com/2ay7l8.

Patronus[19]

Although I sometimes enjoy explaining
that well, yes, my father is a bigfoot,
I've never liked how my mom describes him.
How nerdy-sexy he was, how refined /
surprisingly dreamy Bigfoot could be.
When someone makes you feel like the only
person in the world is you, that's called class.

Because his wife didn't understand him,
Bigfoot came and took my mother away
to see the cherry blossoms one April.
This was done in secret. To know Bigfoot
is to know many things about secrets,
including ways you can hide your own tracks.
I knew that Bigfoot had been in the house

whenever I found a stuffed animal
on a kitchen chair. Bigfoot always left
me animals and Hershey's candy bars
but I don't think that I ever touched him.
I don't remember touching him, although
I'd recognize his profusion of hair,
his brute heart and peculiar skunky scent.

19. http://en.wikipedia.org/wiki/Patronage_in_ancient_Rome
[or tinyurl.com/mzy9dzh] and http://en.wikipedia.org/wiki/Patronus_Charm#Ex
pecto_Patronum_.28Patronus_Charm.29
[or tinyurl.com/5xrhpr].

Every good thing is traced to your father.

You look just like a young Vivian Leigh
your mother says, although Vivian Leigh
has got nothing to do with your father.
You're only eight but you know you're ugly.

She says this as you wait in the kitchen,
one wall with a monster-shaped hole in it:
Your father is very intelligent.

She says this as she considers your small
face, your eyebrows and pale skin, crooked teeth,
thick glasses: *Your father almost swam in
the Olympics.*

Your father, your grandma says years later.
Her eyes turned to the ceiling, she inhales
deeply, then blows smoke from her nose.

Dick Cavett Show, August 19, 1974

Q: Thanks for agreeing to join us today.

A: My pleasure.

Q: Really a thrill to be sitting across from you. Let's start by talking about some of the more recent developments in your long career. Can we discuss your persona?

A: Sure.

Q: Bigfoot. A lot of things to a lot of people.

A: Thanks.

Q: Is that calculated?

A: Well, I don't think of myself as a self-promoter, no.

Q: But here you are.

A: I am here. But I'm pretty much anything they pin on me. Elusive Wild Ape Man. Bucolic Missing-link Bigfoot. Romantic Bigfoot. Invisible Man. I'm black *and* white Jesus. You don't even have to choose. [Laughter, scattered applause.]

The truth is, I don't feel compelled to adopt a label. I never have. But like many other "larger-than-life" characters, I find that people project all sorts of things onto me. Gender issues, race. I've become a marker for regionalism, for class. The whole social construction of nature. I'm *it*, man. The duality of the familiar and the unknown. I am Other.

Q: You are. You are the Other.

I understand you've had run-ins with a number of interesting people.

A. Most were from some distance, sometimes the people weren't even sure what happened. But not always. There were some long-term relationships.

Q: Who are we talking about?

A: I'll never tell.

Q: So to know Bigfoot is to know something about secrets.

A: The majority of these people you've probably never heard of. But I can say there were lots of Indians, and exchanges with a young Teddy Roosevelt. Daniel Boone. John Muir. Ted Bundy. Annie Oakley. Ray Carver. Woody Guthrie. Uhhh . . . Edna St. Vincent Millay. Emerson, of course, and Thoreau. Emily Dickinson. She sometimes left a saucer of milk for me on the step of her greenhouse. Real sweetheart.

Q: Fascinating. You know, I don't think about you in New England.

A: Yeah, I generally don't do a lot of work there, but sometimes I break out of my typical form. New England was like that. A response to that time, to what was happening there. I respected their ethos and wanted to experience it firsthand.

Q: Now your fan base. Traditionally, Native American. Then it shifted, and today it's mostly, what? Mountain people? West Coast hippies?

A: Well, I don't think of myself as a mountain man or a hippie. More a builder of cabins, not particularly concerned with conventional thinking. I would consider myself a Romantic, capital R. But I always appreciate any support for my work.

Q: And there were some important relationships, some complicated ones.

A: You know the P.T. Barnum story. But I won't go into that here. It's all in my book.

Q: Who would you like to have met?

A: Gosh. Buddy Bolden? Walt Whitman? Salinger?

Q: These are very different people.

A: Yeah, but they all speak to a kind of, of—

Q: A kind of Bigfoot spirit.

A: A kind of Bigfoot spirit, yes. I like that.

Q: Maybe I should be your publicist.

A: Maybe you should.

Q: Anyone else?

A: Maybe the wife of Bath.

Q: The Chaucer character?

A: Sure. I figure she'd give me a run for my money. Young Grace Kelly. Young Elizabeth Taylor, although I like her quite a lot now, too, with a little meat on her bones.

Q: You like women.

A: I do. I like women. I like their energy. I like how they smell.

Q: And while you're not political, you are something of a treehugger.

A: That probably comes as no surprise.

Q: Before we go, are there any mysteries you want to settle for us?

A: Only to remind you that I can only speak for myself. I'm certainly not the only one of us out there.

Q: We've been talking with Bigfoot. Thanks again for joining us.

A: Thank you. It was fun.

Zanesville[20]

Sometimes at night, he visits the lions
and tigers burning bright in their cages.

They have that animal understanding.
The big cats, purring fast, will let him reach

between the bars to rub their heavy heads,
to scratch along their silver-whiskered chins

and murmur soft and low, deep in their ears,
Take heart. They never mean to kill their gods.[21]

20. worldwildlife.org/stories/more-tigers-in-american-backyards-than-in-the-wild, or tinyurl.com/mkzvdyp.
21. www.poetryfoundation.org/poem/172943, or tinyurl.com/kvxzhtf.

You spend years there in the kitchen, waiting
for something to happen. Nothing happens.
You sleep with your mother at night. One time
when you're very small, the air hot and still,
you see a shooting star out the window

and this belongs to you because you are
the only one awake. Another time
you wake up on a blue winter morning
to find your mother's long dresser blocking
the door. *I dreamed someone was chasing me,*
she explains.

\- \- \-

Track 4: http://www.youtube.com/watch?v=lH56e2OQD0Y [22]
Any kind of monster is your favorite.

---

22. Or tinyurl.com/meh5v7x.

Timeline

1880 John Stine proposes to his dead wife's sister, Annie. He is a farmer, about forty, she is a spinster midwife. She accepts, telling him, "I will marry you for the sake of the children, but I will never sleep with you."

This sounds strange—would she have said *sleep with* in the nineteenth century?—but these are my grandmother's words. It is 1993 and we are sitting in her house, which smells like cigarettes and meat. The curtains are drawn. Her second husband has been dead for fifteen years. She hasn't gone blind yet.

1962 The Orlons sing *Baby baby when you do the Twist, never never do you get yourself kissed.*

Teenagers everywhere Watusi in response.

1970 Larry Larson proposes to my mother again. They had married in 1955 as teenagers and divorced soon after. She turns him down.

I remember Larry Larson. He was a nice guy. I think he worked on cars.

1917 Anthony Healey, son of Irish immigrants and a cigar maker by trade, dies in California. He had traveled there by train from Michigan, hoping to be cured of his advanced case of tuberculosis. He is survived by a wife and four children, one of whom will be my father's mother. She will live to the age of ninety-six. I will never meet her.

1945 One of my mother's uncles returns home from the war to discover that his wife has contracted the clap. She insists that she got it from a toilet seat. Their marriage survives another forty years.

My mother's father makes it home too, but he and my grand-mother divorce soon after.

1965   John Sebastian writes a song that will go on to be covered by many different singers. The listener is asked, *Do you believe in magic in a young girl's heart? How the music can free her whenever it starts?*

1879   Singer Lillian Russell's infant son dies after his nanny accidentally sticks him with a diaper pin, penetrating his stomach. A successful career and several marriages follow, but Russell doesn't bear another child.

1925   My mother's mother often visits her grandparents' farm, but she dreads sleeping there because she finds the sound of whippoorwills unbearably sad. She will mention this—and imitate a whippoorwill—whenever she talks about her childhood.

1887-91   Jojo the Dog-faced Boy longs for a girl. He longs for a girl with such intensity that many days he can barely look out at his audience, which is enthusiastic and includes a number of women, probably some of whom are kind.

Sometimes he weeps, sometimes he dreams he is reclining on a bed with Lillian Russell. She's wearing a picture hat, a diamond-studded corset, and nothing else. She gently grooms his face with an ivory hairbrush while she hums "Come Down My Evening Star." Her hands are bare, white, small.

Several years later, after the dreams stop, Jojo takes up smoking. He always buys the cigars with Lillian Russell's face on the box.

1977 Larry Larson sometimes comes over and has a beer with my mother. I am upstairs in my room with my 45s and posters of Shaun Cassidy. I don't know where my brother is, but while he is gone I secretly study his copies of *Playboy*.

So much of life is mysterious.

1949 Hank Williams divorces Audrey Sheppard and writes "I'm So Lonesome I Could Cry." It opens with *Hear that lonesome whippoorwill. He sounds too blue to fly.*

My mother sits alone every afternoon at the kitchen table in the trailer, listening to a country-music radio show. My grandmother is at the factory. My grandfather is with his new family. I don't know where my mother's brother is. The show always ends with the Sons of the Pioneers crooning "Tumbling Tumbleweeds." Years later, this song still makes my mother cry.

Your mother pines for Bigfoot many years.
She believes that someday he will come back
for her, for you.

This is a weird way to learn about love.

Track 5: www.youtube.com/watch?v=uHdvWel-fRg [23]
If you're looking for something to look at
while Sarah Vaughan sings, consider googling
images of "shepherd lamb -jesus -pie."
Or better yet "romantic surveillance,"
because you will find much weirder stuff there.

See also www.youtube.com/watch?v=tMcAsfs_DSw [24] and
www.youtube.com/watch?v=_cpX3qrzRfk [25]

Tragedy
Comedy
Tragedy
Comedy
This is how the world works. Or how it should.

23. Or tinyurl.com/7ekugkn.
24. Or tinyurl.com/lcaytvq.
25. Or tinyurl.com/3hgoswy.

They'll say, "Are you married?"
We'll say, "No, man. But you can do the job when you're in town."
For years, you understand this line to mean
they are flirting with the man in the field,
that these little kids are soliciting
a snowman.

There are also a few Bigfoot movies,
including bigfoot porn. This does exist.
While you don't have to watch any of it,
it's clear that you should know it's in the world.

There's actually a lot of porn.

Survival pantoum

Some men will think that
because you're a woman
you don't know anything.
They'll try to take advantage of you.

Because you're a woman,
mechanics will bilk you.
They'll take advantage of you. (One: never go to a dealership.
It's more expensive. Two: get everything in writing first.)

Mechanics are going to try to bilk you
and so is everyone else, so don't forget this:
get everything in writing and never let them know
how much you can pay. It seems like whatever you do

—don't forget this either—
people are pigs. Honest to god
they are, honey. Whatever you do,
never waitress in a family restaurant. The parents are angry

and the kids are pigs and you'll clean up after everyone and lug
heavy trays and those small tips will be impossible to live on. So:
never waitress in a family restaurant. Unless you have to. And then just till
you find a cocktail bar where you can wear good clothes or a nice uniform.

Small tips are hard to live on. Absolutely.
But there is no shame in being poor. And remember:
you can always find a job in a cocktail bar. Trays are light,
drunk businessmen tip well. Just make sure you don't look cheap.

There's no shame in being poor, but there is no excuse for being dirty.
And there absolutely is an art to putting on makeup.

To make sure you don't look cheap, don't highlight every feature.
Don't be afraid to take a good hard look in the mirror,

because the art of putting on makeup
is to make it look like you're not wearing any at all.
And don't forget to look in the mirror
to check the back of your head. People see your hair there too.

Now: when you're afraid, you'll need to look like you're not. At all.
Keep your guard up. Walk fast and lock the doors when you get in.
Look behind you and always check the back seat.
You'll never know what men might do. They can be animals.

You will need to keep your guard up.
You will need to stay in control, because boys will always, always take
whatever they're offered. I'm sorry, but it's the truth. They can be animals.
And no, it isn't fair, but somebody needs to be the responsible one.

So stay in control, and always hold back a little for yourself.
Especially if you go falling in love. Some men will think
this isn't fair
but they don't know anything.

- - -

The story doesn't evolve much over
time. It was pretty much cemented in
college, when Tricia egged you on, her lips
stained purple with cheap wine, bubbles winking
at the brim: *Tell them about your family.*
The truth is that while you were middle-class
by then, your genesis made you seem half-
wild, exotic, to the clean children
of neurosurgeons.

You are the least-scary form of slumming.
They smile, run their hands over your soft fur,
and you smile back with your sharp little teeth.
You always prefer to tell your stories
with a drink in your hand.

I have a drink in my hand
and I'm watching you. Yes.
You there. Trying to
get lost in America, you

fucking hairy Irish fugitive.
You know all the best restaurants
from the Dumpster side. You
carve your scrimshaw in peace,

mourned as Lost at Sea. You
just keep soldiering on, don't you,
knowing that back home
your tapestry's woven
every day, and each day's work
undone every goddamn night.

- - -

In which your mother says there's probably
another bastard Bigfoot girl out there,
child of an earlier secretary.
(Have we established that your mother was
the secretary? Or that Bigfoot is
a real-estate developer? And has
a real son and a real daughter your age?
Because this information's important.)
That Bigfoot kept a photo in his desk
of the other secretary's daughter.
If this is true, she's a couple of years
older than you are.

Your mother thinks they moved to Georgia, but
she's not sure.

The other dream

When I finally
remembered it
it was so familiar
      from the Latin
      something about family
I'd seen it a million times already
and it made me sick.

We stood face to face
      familiar
my bones burned
they groaned with hating him
and my arm swung back
      god I needed some momentum
to slap his face
but as my hand came around
it was so heavy
so slow.

Underwater
weak and silent
where even the violence is clean
is choreographed
is diluted into something
utterly gruesomely harmless

every night
      honest to god
      I really think it was every fucking night
I would swing my hand
with all the strength I could muster
      when I was ten
      when I was twenty
      now that I'm forty-four

and it's always the same:
no matter how hard I push
I am too slow
and the water the distance the blood
between us is too thick.
By the time my palm meets his face
there is no sting left at all.

Hey
I have an idea.
Let's try it again
here in the middle of my kitchen.
I will dry my hands on the dishtowel.

Now you stand *there*.

Make a chart of all your Bigfoot sightings

1) Pine Street, Zanesville, Ohio, 1973. Your mother tells you to answer the door when Bigfoot knocks and to say that she is in the bathtub. Bigfoot takes you to lunch. He eats a patty melt, drinks a chocolate milkshake, and leaves you again at the front door.

2) Vending-machine room, Franklin County courthouse, Columbus, Ohio, 1980. You are eleven, sporting a homemade haircut and a dress you picked out at KMart because of the matching shawl trimmed in acrylic lace. You are reading a paperback screenplay of the TV show *Eight Is Enough*. Bigfoot walks in wearing a necktie and a white dress shirt, carrying his suit jacket and a tiny can of V8. You have been told that he is tall, and he is. He announces himself by saying *Hi [your name here], I'm your father.* His legal obligation is now complete.

You are both wearing thick glasses with dark brown frames. You have his crooked incisors. You are trying to figure out how else you belong to him as he talks about how he recently went deep-sea fishing with Jack Nicklaus, the golfer, and caught a marlin. He asks if you know what a marlin is. You do.

On his way out, Bigfoot pulls a checkbook from his suit jacket and tears off the left corner from the first check. You now have Bigfoot's address and telephone number. *Next time you're in Columbus, give me a buzz,* he says. When you get home, tape this scrap to your bedroom wall. It will stay there for years. You and your mother will never speak of it.

3) Dalt's restaurant, Worthington, Ohio, 1988. You call and ask Bigfoot to lunch, which seems like a very adult thing to do. You wear a flippy floral skirt, a thrift-store sweatshirt, black leggings, magenta Chuck Taylors. Your hair is permed, which is okay because everyone's hair is permed. Lunch is unremarkable, other than that you

are nervous and can't find him when you first arrive at the restaurant, which is full of middle-aged white bigfoots dining alone.

You order french fries and a Coke because you might have to pay for your own food and you don't have much money. Bigfoot has a patty melt and a chocolate milkshake, then walks you out. He shakes your hand and drives off in what you think was a black Lincoln Town Car.

You, another brown-eyed bigfoot

When you are fourteen,
cultivate a friendship
with a bigfoot's younger sister.
He doesn't notice you at school
and he's never at home
when you visit, but their house
smells good, like soap only softer,
and you imagine he smells
like this, only more so.
You fill your pink lungs with his smell
in their kitchen, their bathroom,
inside their car. Sometimes
between classes you will pick up
his scent over the ordinary tang
of sweat and fruity chapstick
and your knees will go weak.

This morning you find him
on sweetrussianbrides.com.
He's gray now, says he's
easygoing. Still a big guy.
A loaf of grocery-store
bread is jauntily tucked under his arm
like a football, like how
the latest baby might be carried
by a man with too many children.
In all caps, the website promises
*YOU DON'T NEED
RUSSIAN MARRIAGE AGENCY
TO FIND YOUR BELOVED.*

Koko turns a copy of Keats's death
mask over in her warm and capable
paws. Fingering the noble nose and full
mouth, the thick clump of wet eyelashes, she
signs *pretty*. She signs *trouble* and *cry*.

The German *sehnsucht* is such a good word.

It understands that sometimes the longing
means more than the longed-for thing itself.

Track 6: www.youtube.com/watch?v=GOlkRP6zNlY [26]

Cut off what's left of your perm. Study up
on the ways you can tie a scarf, on how
to bone a fish at the table. Buy a
thrift-store coat with a fox collar. Tell one
boy in the darkness that penises are
the same kind of soft as horses' noses.
(You've stolen this line from Esther Williams.)

Do a lot of things in fear. Wish later
that you'd done more.

- - -

I was a flower of the mountain [27] *yes when I put the rose in my hair like
the bigfoot girls or shall I wear a red yes and how he kissed me by the
kitchen window and I thought well as well him as another and then I
asked him with my eyes to ask again yes and then he asked me would I
yes to say yes my mountain flower and first I put my arms around him
yes and drew him down to me so he could feel my breasts all perfume yes
and his heart was going like mad and yes I said yes I will Yes.*

26. Or tinyurl.com/kbjquow.
27. www.youtube.com/watch?v=yNTlDesrY3w, or tinyurl.com/msy92k.

Love story no. six[28]

Dear god I have been wife to five husbands
and I've known plenty of other men and

I've seen a lot of this world. However
I've never seen reason not to gather

one more little rosebud. Just look at me—
I'm no old woman. I deserve to be

happy. Heaven knows it's not good to live
alone, always tending your own garden.

It's right to sow the occasional stray
seed, sometimes be refreshed in a strange stream.

Where was I? I was on the bank and saw
this beast—an ugly brute, but nothing a

good suit and a bath couldn't fix. He trailed
me home, waited at the gate. He failed to

take no for an answer. So I said yes.
And why wouldn't I? Those big pleading eyes.

Poor thing came when called. I tossed him a beet
and watched it break bloody between his teeth

—crowded, sharp, double rowed—then admired his
strong jaws and legs, ready sex. Bowing low

he took an apple right from my hand. Tame.
I've no choice but to love him. He needs me.

---

28. http://classiclit.about.com/library/bl-etexts/gchaucer/bl-gchau-can-bath.htm,
or tinyurl.com/4j84ac.

Track 7: www.youtube.com/watch?v=ajwnmkEqYpo [29]
You do and you do and it never stops.

- - -

Track 8: http://vimeo.com/39267368[30]

Hoard the last packet of cake mix for the
Easy-Bake oven, knowing there won't be
any more. Fall in love with whole decades
that took place before you were born and with
anyone unavailable to you.
Get teary thinking that your Kodachrome
dress will wear out one day and where will you
be then?

Beyond these things, on the continuum
of lost animals, you pass for normal.
Listen to a bunch of Elliott Smith
when you want to feel really terrible.
Now there's a guy who had a baboon heart.

30. Or tinyurl.com/8urghzy.

1900   Excerpt from a letter to explorer Robert Peary from his wife, Josephine. We are in Greenland:

I have looked out for Allakasingwah and your boy & allowed them in the cabin with Marie. It is a great concession for me to make. . . . It cut me like a knife to hear her tell Marie all about you . . . to think she had been in your arms, has received your caresses, has heard your love-cries, I could die at the thought. . . . Have you, my husband, ever thought what these years have been to me since I bade you farewell? During these hungry years I have been consoling myself . . . with the thought that it was just as hard for you, & I must be brave for your sake. . . . On reaching Etah I find you have probably never given me a thought & a creature scarcely human has the power to make you forget everything except her. Oh my love, why do I live?

But there, I did not mean to give way to my feelings.

His wife, bundled up in her Arctic furs:
http://en.wikipedia.org/wiki/File:Josephine_Peary_portrait_1892.jpg [31]

His lover, stripped nude, Mother of the Seals:
www.archive.org/stream/northwardovergre01pear#page/500/mode/2up [32]

31. Or tinyurl.com/otyzqp7.
32. Or tinyurl.com/m2bp9zb.

I will arise and go now[33] and fold the load of laundry.
I'll fold and think about the deep heart's core.

That's nice, that place with no mouth, no words.
Warmed in the dark, in the inside of the machine.
There is so much already lost—gardenia corsages,
that transatlantic accent every movie star once had,
whole languages and useful words like *retard*.

All of us long for peace I think, dropping slow, stooping
to take the size-six underpants in hand, to lay them
on the underwear pile. Jared saw a coyote
trotting down the sidewalk just last summer, past
the pigeon-breasted Victorians with their enclosed courtyards.
Why were we surprised to remember that animals live nearby?
Why do we love deer so much, and how they'll stare right back
           wherever we might meet them
                      on the roadway or the pavement
                      before they run

Before, when people asked about Father's
Day, you would say it doesn't make you feel
anything. Some people celebrate it,
but it simply doesn't apply to you.
Like a Jewish holiday, you told them.
After you marry a Jew, this sounds weird.

Get a friend request from a half-sister.
Accept. Set the DVR to record
her appearance on the *Dog Whisperer.*
Don't make any plans to meet each other.

Long winter

These gorgeous kids
all dirty-faced and smart-mouthed
begging for Sprite and shoving
more garbage, more candy money under their beds
while beside the pool breathing warm chlorine
you are daydreaming about tea parties
and the inner workings of men
who wear silk slippers and powdered wigs.
I've decided not to spend the day studying the wallpaper.
I already know how it goes
        it goes yellow stripe flower spray flower spray
        flower spray yellow stripe
and to treat myself to the act of cleaning up with trash bags
instead of Q-Tips.
I'm enjoying the smell of my own sweat.
We don't fill enough trash bags, smell enough sweat.

There is no connected center.
See over there: That goldfish has been doing laps in solitary
for almost three years now but he's fine.

That woman on the bus talked too loud
and every word meant something
in Chinese except when it meant something in English.
She went something something something
West Side something something
bar mitzvah something something something temple
but we were connected to her
we were straining to hear
hoping she would say Disneyland, Charles Dickens, Filet-o-Fish, IUD
as long as it wasn't more on the imagery of ecstatic motherhood.

Beyond these walls between the houses
stretch unshoveled sidewalks and
telephone lines that I would like to describe as silvery
but they're not pretty and we don't even need them anymore.
We've hung our satellites and
made cell-phone towers look like trees
and somehow we all know our places, past and present:
Your chair, my end of the couch
My lime, my sad guitar
your Beethoven, your aliens, my séance, our Bigfoot.
My grandmother's cheap white coffee cup
chipped saucer, cheery Pall Mall box
type dropped to white on red, its own blessing
Per aspera ad astra, in hoc signo vinces.
Any of us can tell at a glance: my burrito.
We all know what to do:
You call I answer I call you answer
You call I never answer
You don't call I don't answer.

Kale Peary, speaking to a reporter,
talks about his father and his sled dogs:
http://articles.latimes.com/1987-09-13/news/mn-7456_1_
american-explorer-peary [34]

As the Soul Hovers over the Body, Reluctantly Parting with Life

Realize the need for a ritual for *What to Do as Your Father Lies Dying in the Hospice*

This after hours of aimlessly casting about your office. Go to the debriefing meeting about the conference. Hate meetings. Hate conferences. Hate people

Go home and pour a glass of wine. Pour another. Stare into the middle space. Tongue your dead tooth. The tooth feels alive, it looks fine doesn't it? Well apparently it isn't. *Maybe Tooth 28 suffered an early trauma,* the dentist said last week, explaining internal resorption. *Maybe you got hit in the face with a ball when you were six and it's showing up now for some reason*

Sometimes, she added, moving on, *the body just turns on itself*

Resist calling this the death watch or the Death Watch or the Bigfoot Death Watch. Resist abbrev. to BFDW. Briefly consider *abbreviate.* Realizing you don't know what to call this, burst into tears again

Announce to the family: *We are driving to the ocean*

1) Drive to the ocean, first taking a detour to a Mexican restaurant you have heard good things about, because you will be angry with the children if they complain of hunger on the beach

The waitress tells a ghost story

You could call this *liminal space*

Just this week you dreamed your grandmother briefly returned from
the dead to buy contact lenses, which she'd heard are much improved.
You waited together for her appointment. Her eyes were cloudier than
they had been in life but she was obviously still your grandmother

She is still your grandmother

2) Use your phone to take a photo of the coin as it lies on the table at
the haunted restaurant

Your father had sent your mother out during her lunch hour to buy
the coin, minted in celebration of the 1968 Olympics, as a gift for your
brother, who turned eight at the end of that summer. Your father was
trying to win over your brother, who already had his own absent bigfoot.
Your brother gave you the coin years later, shrugging *Maybe you want
this*. It's a satisfying size and weight. An Aztec, balancing on one foot,
dances on one side

There is gravity in it

Your children seem concerned that by hurling the coin into the Atlantic,
you will be throwing away their inheritance. *It's worth twenty dollars,*
you assure them. You've looked it up on eBay. You know this

At the restaurant, your son suggests you read "The Negro Speaks
of Rivers." Hughes and his father were also estranged, your son explains.
Hughes wrote this poem as he pondered the Mississippi, on his way
to visit him. The visit didn't go well, your son adds

*Except for the physical and spiritual dimensions, the subjective "I" and
the "river" read the same*

3) Belly full, darkness descended, separate from your family. The din allows you be lonely alone. The tide is out. The ocean invites you to walk its floor

4) Walk the floor of the ocean until the ocean begins

5) Pull out the coin, warm from your pocket. Appreciate the transfer of heat from body to object: the surrogate you, the phantom you

6) Feet shoulder-width apart   shift your weight   wind your arm back   follow through

7) Note how the coin fumbles as you release. You are a poor athlete

8) Regret this for an instant

9) Forgive yourself immediately

10) Watch for the glint arcing out over the water but it's too dark, too dark

Saying *I was created by a world-*
ly charismatic raconteur is just
a different way of saying *My bigfoot*
was a confidence man.

Eventually Facebook tells you Bigfoot
is dead, because Facebook is like that. You
consider a photo of him with his
family, in the woods. You were born between
the blonde girl and the squirmy dark-haired boy.
You are the little shadow in the leaves.

His obit mentions Evel Knievel,
the marlin, his high school swimming record
from 1952, his personal helicopter,
golf, the blonde girl, the squirmy boy, but not

you. Consider the concept of freedom
from your biggest monster. That night your mom
(who has seen Bigfoot's obituary)
emails to say *You're a better person*
than any of them.

They'll text you after his body is deep
in the ground, because it would be awkward
if you came to the funeral. You weren't
listed in the will. You never needed
to learn any of Cordelia's lines,
and not any of Edmund's lines either.
You've had your inheritance all along.

Consider illegitimate versus
legitimate people, legitimate

versus illegitimate grief, phantom
limbs, pain. Consider the loss of phantom
limbs and pain, of those absences that have
presence. Consider *phantom.* (*Phantasm,*
for ghost, also *fantasy.*)
                              Now Google
Duane Michals's photo *Man as Spirit* and
make it your new profile picture.

- - -

- - -

Once you start breaking out in hives when you
drink red wine, learn to prefer gin instead.

Buy a birdfeeder and, relying on
things you learned twenty years ago from a
boyfriend who was avoiding his thesis,
teach your kids to recognize common birds.

- - -

Become a beekeeper.

Visitation: Cape Cod [35]

Go to the forest, listen and realize
there's no good reception. You'll need to wait
maybe a long time if you want answers.
When a red fox walks into your shins, ask

for forgiveness in an English accent.
You hope this somehow conveys your respect.
The fox knows mercy and invention and
music in ways you never will. But while

his life is pretty good, it's not worth one
thousand of yours. Foxes tell good stories
but they exaggerate. Admire his sharp
face, fine coat. Back away in deference.

As he trots west, nosing the pond's dark edge,
　　　look to the chickadee gripping your thumb,
　　　eating seeds out of the palm of your hand.

---

35. http://yearsrisingmaryoliver.blogspot.com/2010/10/straight-talk-from-fox.html,
　　or tinyurl.com/lezqgel.

Another[36] prelude[37]

Yes I wander lonely
as a bigfoot because
bigfoot are lonely
by nature. Placid days
stalking solitary through
the icy brooks and orchards,
the corn, bright and green,
skirting the disappointing
village and its somewhat
creepy bed and breakfast.
I sometimes crouch
on the other side of the wisteria,
fingering the blossoms,
purple fragrance falling,
and breathe in the smell
of the bacon, the mini blueberry
muffins served on the termite-
infested veranda. The tasteful perfume
of women who used to be mothers
here with their faded husbands
for a weekend of hikes and bike rides
and afternoon glasses of wine,
trying to remind themselves how
to be together again. Their experience,
their desires, their apprehensions—
I blush for them all. In these moments,
soft-sauntering away, I feel confident.
It's knowing I'm unfit for this scale
that throws me into despair.
Wailing, eating my own shit. Unable
to partake of this day's pleasure.

---

36. www.poetryfoundation.org/poetrymagazine/poem/239964, or tinyurl.com/3ot3zkd.
37. http://en.wikipedia.org/wiki/The_Prelude, or tinyurl.com/1rn9378.

Struggling to find the right words,
except to say I'm glad these clouds
are always with me.

The you at the table is you. You are eight. You are also the table, your mother, the carpet. You are the chipped wooden and new plastic cabinets and the faucet and the sink wiped clean. You are the window and the three stairs that lead to the door. You are the door. And you are Bigfoot, who walks past the window you, through the door you, and picks up your mother you. The Bigfoot who carries her past the peonies and into the woods. The woods that are also you.

About the author

Amy Pickworth's poems have been published in CATACOMB; *Forklift, Ohio;* H_NGM_N; *Ink Node;* New Ohio Review; *Smartish Pace; and* Two Serious Ladies. *She lives in Providence, Rhode Island.* **amypickworth.com**

About the press

Orange Monkey Publishing is a small press based in the Inland Empire of Southern California. Started in May of 2012, the press has grown to include authors such as Nikia Chaney, Michelle Bonczek, F. Daniel Rzicznek, L.I. Henley, Raul Zurita and S.Marie Clay. We hold one book contest a year and the rest of our books are found via scouts. For more information, please visit **orangemonkeypublishing.com**

and here...

tinyurl.com/m6tajyh

✕ *and also here.*